COPYCAT RECIPES COOKBOOK

The complete step by step cookbook with most popular recipes from american restaurant, easy to make and fast to cook

SCOTT CLOUTIER

Table of Contents

Introduction

It is a good idea to try something new each day to get out of your comfort zone. Maybe daily takeout's have been your life but try testing recipes for a chance to find out whether you have been cutting yourself from advantages. There is no need to do unique things every day. Just by applying different approaches to your daily activities, slowly over the course of time, you can change your life for the better. This book is just what you need to switch from takeout to homemade meals.

Though none of the recipes are difficult and all of them are easy to manipulate and make, cooking in the kitchen will steadily improve your skills. Sometimes, our motivation drains out if we are working hard on something that we don't want. These restaurant meals can give you the drive to continue with this learning process by providing you with a happy meal.

Cooking and food are one way to bring family and friends together and spend time with each other. There should be a family meal at least once a day. Improve your family meals and inspire other members to join you in your new hobby.

You can invite multiple friends and enjoy their never-ending compliments on your dish as well.

People are becoming more aware these days of the dangers of careless eating. A perfect diet can increase the years in your life. That is worth some hard work in the kitchen. Take outs and restaurants are extremely unhealthy, and healthy food tends to be very expensive. So, get the best of both worlds by eating takeout foods once in a while to get your health routine started.

Healthy eating should be necessary for not only your life, but the life of your friends and family as well. Inspire them with your cooking skills and motivate them to make their lives healthier as well.

Try cooking your favorite dishes from high-end restaurants to make breakfast, lunch, and dinner more fun and diverse. Put something new on the table and let people comment or two to give you advice. Undoubtedly, they will leave being extremely impressed by you and your ability to make various foods.

Restaurants don't care about being health conscious. Their food is laced with high levels of sodium, sugar, and oils. Nutritious meals will put you a step closer to a healthy life you always wanted. You can do that now by making copycat meals at your home.

What's great is that you don't have to drive or walk for hours to be at a certain place to eat—the most comfortable area is in your home. Many people will prefer eating in rather than out, but not many people are confident in their cooking. By applying some skills in your kitchen, you will end up with a happy day. Many proven delicious recipes in this book will give you step by step instructions so that your dish turns out perfect.

Good luck and Happy Cooking!

Chapter 1. Essential (Most Common Ingredient and Tools)

1. Fish

Knowing how to choose fresh fish is a skill that all cooks should have. Fresh fish should smell like clean water. The fish's eyes should be bright and clear, and the gills should be a rich, bright red. If it smells bad or looks discolored, don't buy it.

2. Vegetables

Take the time to inspect each vegetable before you buy it. Look for crunchy, meaty, and brightly colored vegetables. Avoid those that are shriveled, bruised, moldy, or stained.

• The asparagus must have straight, compact stalks with closed tips.

• Beans that are colorful and crunchy are best to select.

• Celery stalks should have crunchy ribs.

• Cucumbers should be firm and have no soft spots.

• Wilted or brown-spotted peas should be avoided.

• Crisp, bright-colored peppers should be chosen.

• Spinach leaves should be crunchy and free of moisture.

3. Food Presentation

Whenever you go to a fantastic restaurant, the vibes around that place become as important as the quality of the food served in determining whether or not you have a fulfilling experience. Remember that food presentation and table setting are of the highest value when serving a restaurant imitator meal.

Chapter 2. Breakfast recipes

4. Glazed Donuts from Krispy Kreme

These original glazed donuts are light and chewy and a good way to get anyone out of bed in the morning. Who can resist a Krispy Kreme recipe copycat?

Preparation Time: 30 minutes

Cooking Time: 120 minutes

Servings: 24

Difficulty Level: Medium

Ingredients:

- For the Donut Batter,

- Five cups of flour (all-purpose)

- Four and a half teaspoons of instant yeast

- One and a half cup of low fat or whole milk

- One tsp. of salt

- Two eggs (large in size)

- One-third cup of warm water (40-46C or 105-115F)

- Half cup of granulated sugar

- One-third cup of soft butter/shortening (nearly 75g)

- Canola oil (needed for frying)

- For the Donut glaze,

- Five-seven tbsps. of evaporated milk

- Half cup of melted butter

- Two teaspoons of vanilla

- Two cups of sugar (powdered)

Directions

Take a standing mixer and mix yeast and lukewarm water. Keep it undisturbed for nearly five minutes until it dissolves.

In the meantime, heat milk in a medium-sized microwave-safe bowl for two minutes. Allow it to cool.

Now, add eggs, milk, salt, sugar, two cups flour, butter, or shortening to the yeast bowl.

Mix all the ingredients properly at a medium speed. Then, pour three cups flour and keep mixing the dough.

As it is done, take a large-sized greased bowl and place the dough in it. Cover the bowl loosely with a cloth and keep it in a warm place for nearly one-two hours. By doing so, the dough will rise.

Sprinkle flour on a clean surface and then roll the dough to a thickness of about a quarter inch. Start cutting the donuts with a cookie cutter or donut cutter of about one inch. Allow it to stand for ten minutes.

Meanwhile, pour canola oil (minimum three inches high) into a large-sized saucepan and place it on medium heat. Heat the oil until it is 375 degrees.

Drop a few donuts into the hot oil very carefully. Turn the donuts once and fry for three minutes till they are golden brown in color. Keep the fried donuts on paper towels.

As soon as you are done with frying, melt butter in a bowl (microwave safe).

Remove the bowl and add vanilla extract and powdered sugar into it. Keep stirring until all the ingredients mix evenly.

Next, you need to add evaporated milk until you get a perfect consistency.

Now dip all the donuts in the glaze. Allow them to drip on a rack. Mouthwatering glazed donuts are ready to be served.

Nutrition:

- Calories: 228

- Protein: 3g

- Carbs: 35g

- Fat: 8g

- Fiber: 1g

5. Biscuits and Sausage Gravy From Bob Evans

Biscuits served with hot sausage gravy are a sure way to stay satisfied until your next meal.

Preparation Time: 5 minutes

Cooking Time: 7 minutes

Servings: 2

Difficulty Level: Easy

Ingredients:

- 2-3 tbsps. of flour (all-purpose flour can be used)

- Warm biscuits

- A quarter-pound of bulk pork sausage

- One and a quarter cups of whole milk

- Two tbsps. of butter

- One-eighth tsp. of pepper

- A quarter tsp. of salt

Directions:

Firstly, take a clean and small skillet for cooking the sausage on medium heat. Cook till the pink color of the sausage is gone.

Quickly add the butter and start heating until it melts.

Now, add flour, pepper, and salt. Keep stirring until it blends nicely.

Slowly add milk and stir continuously. Let it boil, stir, and cook for nearly two minutes till it thickens. Serve with warm biscuits.

Note: For enhancing the flavor of your gravy, you may add fresh herbs such as parsley. If you want, then you can substitute whole milk with skim milk or heavy cream.

Nutrition

- Calories: 337

- Protein: 10g

- Carbs: 8g

- Fat: 27g

- Fiber: 1g

Chapter 3. Breakfast Recipes Part 2

6. Blueberry Oat Squares from Starbucks

These wholesome bars are just like Starbucks blueberry squares (if not better!) My favorite thing about this recipe is the oatmeal base/crumble.

Preparation Time: 30 minutes

Cooking Time: 45 minutes

Servings: 24

Difficulty Level: Easy

Ingredients:

- Four teaspoons of corn starch

- One-third cup of orange juice

- Half a cup of sugar

- Three cups of fresh blueberries

- Three-fourth cup of softened butter

- Half a tsp. of baking soda

- Half a tsp. of salt

- One cup of brown sugar

- One cup all-purpose flour

- Two cups of oats (quick-cooking)

Directions:

Take a saucepan and add orange juice, sugar, and blueberries. Bring them to a boil. Then reduce the heat and simmer for about ten minutes until tender. Whisk in the corn starch and then boil. Stir for about one minute until it thickens. Put the plastic wrap on the surface directly and refrigerate for about one hour to one day at maximum before serving.

Take a large bowl and add baking soda, salt, brown sugar, flour, and oats. Stir together. Cut the butter in a way that it forms a crumbly mixture. Put aside one and a half cups of the crumbs and spread the rest of the crumbs into the bottom of a greased pan (9 by 13 inch) evenly.

Then, over the base, spread the blueberry mixture. Take the Portion of the crumbly mixture that you have put aside earlier, and then crumble it over the blueberry mixture.

Bake for about 40 to 45 minutes until lightly golden. Allow it to cool down completely on the racks itself as it is easier to cut it down when it is nicely cooled. You can cover it lightly and refrigerate for about two days maximum, or you can even do heavy wrapping using a heavy-duty foil and freeze it for about two weeks.

Nutrition

- Calories: 160.2

- Carbs: 25.1g

- Protein: 1.7g

- Fat: 6.3g

- Fiber: 1.3g

7. Hash Browns from McDonald's

Hash Browns are deliciously tasty. These shredded potato hash brown patties are prepared, so they're fluffy on the inside and crispy and toasty on the outside.

Preparation Time: 20 minutes

Cooking Time: 10 minutes

Servings: 24

Difficulty Level: Easy

Ingredients:

- Two large-sized eggs (beaten lightly)

- Three large-sized potatoes (peeled properly, approximately two lbs.)

- Two tbsps. all-purpose flour

- One tbsp. grated onion

- Half a tsp. baking powder

- One tsp. of salt

- For frying – Vegetable oil

28

Directions:

Grate the potatoes thoroughly after peeling them. If there is any liquid, drain it. Now, add the following ingredients together – baking powder, salt, flour, onion, and eggs.

Take a frying pan and place it on medium-high flame. Add oil to the pan and cover one-eighth inch at the bottom.

Take tablespoonfuls of the batter and add it to the oil. Then use a spatula to form them into patties. Keep frying them until the patties become golden-brown in color. Turn them once in between.

Serve the hash browns immediately.

Note: Serve these with applesauce or smoked salmon.

Nutrition:

- Calories: 257

- Carbs: 41g

- Protein: 6g

- Fat: 8g

- Fiber: 5g

Chapter 4. Brunch recipes

8. Zuppa Toscana Soup

Creamy Zuppa Toscana recipe, full of crumbled sausage, crispy bacon, and tender potatoes in a creamy broth! Make this Olive Garden Soup right at home!

Preparation Time: 23 minutes

Cooking Time: 12 minutes

Servings: 10

Difficulty Level: Hard

Ingredients:

- Ground hot sausage (1 lb.)

- Garlic cloves (3)

- Medium onion (1)

- Flour (1 tbsp.)

- Chicken broth (2 - 32 oz. cartons)

- Russet potatoes (6)

- Heavy cream (1 cup)

- Kale pieces (6 cups - torn)

Directions:

Crumble and toss the sausage into a large soup pot using the medium temperature setting. Once browning, mince and add in the diced onion and garlic. After the onions are translucent, sprinkle them using the flour and mix in the broth. Wait for it to boil.

Wash the potatoes thoroughly and cut them into halves lengthwise (¼-inch slices). Toss them into the boiling pot and simmer until done (20 min.).

Set the heat to low. Mix in the heavy cream and toss the kale into the pot. Simmer for about five minutes, occasionally stirring before serving.

Nutrition

- Calories: 216

- Carbs: 23.5g

- Protein: 19g

- Fat: 13g

9. Chicken Piccata

Chicken piccata is nothing more than chicken breast cutlets, dredged in flour, browned, and served with a sauce of butter, lemon juice, capers, and either stock or white wine. It can be prepared in 20 minutes or less and is so easy and delicious it should be part of every home cook's repertoire.

Preparation Time: 13minutes

Cooking Time: 27 minutes

Servings: 5

Difficulty Level: Hard

Ingredients:

- Pounded chicken breasts (4/0.25-inch thickness/2 lb.)

- Onion (1 small)

- Sun-dried tomatoes in strips (10)

- Garlic (1 minced)

- Chicken broth (1 tbsp.)

- Juiced lemon (2 tbsp./half of 1)

- Rinsed capers (.25 cup)

- Butter (3 tbsp.)

- Heavy cream (.33 cup)

- For Frying: Olive oil (4 tbsp.)

- Black pepper and salt (as desired)

Directions:

Pound the chicken with a mallet and dust it using pepper and salt.

Pour the oil into a pan and fry the chicken using the med-high temperature setting (5-8 min. per side). Take them from the skillet and put them in a covered container for now.

35

Toss in the onion, tomatoes, and garlic into the same pan to sauté until they are a golden brown (1-2 min.). Whisk in the lemon juice, chicken broth, and capers. Scoot the browned bits in the pan and continue cooking them for 10-15 minutes (med-low) until it's reduced by about half in volume.

Once the sauce is thickened, take the pan off of the burner and mix in the butter until it's melted. Then mix in the cream.

Heat the mixture thoroughly and combine with the chicken to reheat. Cover the chicken in sauce and serve.

Note: You can also use one to two tablespoons of the sun-dried tomato oil for part of the olive oil for a flavor change.

Nutrition

- Calories: 130

- Carbs: 36g

- Protein: 14.5g

- Fat: 5.4g

Chapter 5. Starters & Entrees recipes

10.   Blueberry Syrup

You will need something to go over those delicious pancakes and French toast you made earlier, so try this version of Cracker Barrel's blueberry syrup.

Preparation Time: 10 minutes

Cooking Time: 30 minutes

Servings: 3

Ingredients:

- 2 cups blueberries

- ½ cup sugar

- 1 cup water

- 1 tablespoon cornstarch

Directions:

Combine the cornstarch with 2 tablespoons of water in a small bowl. Whisk until no longer clumpy and set aside.

Combine the water, blueberries, and sugar in a saucepan. Bring the mixture to a boil, then reduce the heat and simmer for about 10 minutes or until it has reduced a bit. Stir in the cornstarch and whisk until well combined. Continue to simmer and stir until the sauce has thickened.

When it has reached a syrup-like consistency, remove from heat. You can mix with an immersion blender if you choose.

Serve with pancakes or waffles.

Nutrition:

- Calories 215

- Protein 25

- Carbs 16

- Fat 5

11. Olive Garden Stuffed Chicken Marsala

Don't forget your marsala wine for this savory-sweet Olive Garden classic recipe!

Preparation Time: 25 minutes

Cooking Time: 45 minutes

Servings: 4

Difficulty Level: Easy

Ingredients:

Chicken

- 4 boneless skinless chicken breasts

- ¾ cup all-purpose flour

- Salt and pepper to taste

- ½ cup olive oil

- Parsley, chopped, for garnish

Stuffing

- ½ cup smoked provolone or gouda cheese, shredded

- ½ pound mozzarella cheese, shredded

- ¼ cup parmesan cheese, grated

- ½ cup breadcrumbs

- 1 teaspoon fresh garlic, minced

- 1 teaspoon red pepper flakes

- 2 tablespoons sun-dried tomatoes, patted dry and roughly chopped

- 3 green onions, thinly sliced

- ¾ cup sour cream

Sauce

- 1 yellow onion, sliced into strings

- ¼ dry marsala wine

- 1 cup heavy cream

- ¾ pound button mushrooms, thinly sliced

Directions:

Combine all stuffing ingredients in a bowl. Set aside and preheat oven to 350°F.

Make two slices at the thickest part of each chicken breast in order to butterfly it. Turn the chicken over and lay it flat. Cover with wax paper and pound to about ¼–½ inches in thickness.

Stuff each chicken breast, but do not overfill. Coat the chicken in salt, pepper, and flour.

Cook the chicken in olive oil in a large skillet over medium-high heat. Once cooked, transfer to a baking dish and bake for 15–20 minutes or until the inside is cooked through.

Using the same large skillet, cook the onions in the chicken drippings for about 2 minutes. Add the mushrooms and continue to sauté for about 5 more minutes.

Deglaze by adding wine to the skillet. Heat the wine until lightly bubbling to reduce it. Continue to cook until the sauce turns brown.

Heat the heavy cream in the microwave for 20 seconds. Pour it into the pan and heat until it bubbles slightly. Reduce heat to low and simmer for 5 minutes. Remove from heat when the sauce is a rich brown color.

Serve the sauce over the stuffed chicken and complement the meal with mashed potatoes, if desired. Sprinkle with chopped parsley.

Nutrition:

- Calories: 930

- Carbs: 33g

- Fat: 58g

- Protein: 74g

Chapter 6. Main Courses Recipes

12.Chicken Giardino

A healthy alternative to alfredo, Chicken Giardino boasts a garden-full of vegetables and grilled chicken topped with a delicious sauce.

Preparation Time: 10 minutes

Cooking Time: 20 minutes

Servings: 4

Difficulty Level: Medium

Ingredients:

Sauce

- 1 tablespoon butter

- ¼ teaspoon dried thyme

- ½ teaspoon fresh rosemary, finely chopped

- 1 teaspoon garlic pepper seasoning

- 1 tablespoon cornstarch

- ¼ cup chicken broth

- ¼ cup water

- ¼ cup white wine

- 1 tablespoon milk

- 1 teaspoon lemon juice

- Salt and pepper

Chicken

- 2 pounds boneless skinless chicken breasts

- ¼ cup extra virgin olive oil

- 2 small rosemary sprigs

- 1 clove garlic, finely minced

- Juice of ½ lemon

Vegetables

- ¼ cup extra-virgin olive oil

- ½ bunch fresh asparagus (remove the bottom inch of stem, cut the remainder into 1-inch pieces)

- 1 zucchini, julienned

- 1 summer squash, julienned

- 2 roma tomatoes, cut into ½-inch pieces

- ½ red bell pepper, julienned

- 1 cup broccoli florets, blanched

- ½ cup frozen peas

- 1 cup spinach, cut into ½-inch pieces

- ½ cup carrot, julienned

- 1 pound farfalle pasta (bow ties)

Directions

In a saucepan, melt the butter over medium heat. Add the thyme, garlic, pepper, and rosemary. Whisk together and cook for 1 minute.

In a mixing bowl, mix together the chicken broth, water, wine, milk, and lemon juice. Slowly pour in the cornstarch and whisk constantly until it has dissolved.

Pour the mixture into the saucepan. Whisk well and then bring to a boil. Season with salt and pepper to taste, then remove from heat.

Prepare the chicken by cutting into strips width-wise. In a mixing bowl, combine the olive oil, rosemary, garlic, and lemon juice. Marinate the chicken for at least 30 minutes.

Heat ¼ cup of olive oil over medium-high heat in a saucepan. Cook the chicken strips until the internal temperature is 165°F. Add the vegetables to the saucepan and sauté until cooked.

Prepare the pasta according to package instructions. Drain. Add the pasta and pasta sauce to the sauté pan.

Toss to thoroughly coat pasta and chicken in sauce. Serve.

Nutrition:

- Calories: 323

- Carbs: 19g

- Fat: 22g

- Protein: 32g

13. Chicken and Sausage Mixed Grill

The perfect start-of-summer dish that will make you whip out the BBQ and prepare for grilling season.

Preparation Time: 10 minutes

Cooking Time: 35 minutes

Servings: 4

Difficulty Level: Easy

Ingredients:

Marinade

- 2 teaspoons red pepper oil

- 2 tablespoons fresh rosemary, chopped

- ½ cup fresh lemon juice

- 1 teaspoon salt

- 3 bay leaves, broken into pieces

- 2 large garlic cloves, pressed

- ¼ cup extra-virgin olive oil

- Freshly shredded parmesan cheese, for serving

Skewers

- 2 pounds skinless, boneless chicken breasts

- 1 pound Italian sausage links, mild

- 1 pint cherry tomatoes

- 1 bag bamboo skewers, soaked in water for at least 30 minutes

- 3 lemons, halved

- 2 rosemary sprigs

Directions

To make the marinade, mix pepper oil, rosemary, lemon juice, salt, bay leaves, and pressed garlic in a baking dish.

Cut the chicken breasts in half lengthwise. Pierce each chicken piece with a skewer and thread through. Add a cherry tomato at the end of the skewer. Coat each skewer with the marinade. Marinate for at least 3 hours in the refrigerator.

Preheat oven to 350°F. Bake sausage for 20 minutes. Let cool, then cut into 3 pieces.

Grill chicken until completely cooked. Place sausages on skewers. Grill.

Serve by garnishing with rosemary, lemon, and cherry tomatoes on a platter. Sprinkle with freshly shredded parmesan, if desired.

Nutrition:

- Calories: 234

- Carbs: 32g

- Fat: 29g

Protein: 37g

Chapter 7. Mains

14. Wendy's Black Bean Chili

A chili that is best prepared with fresh vegetables, but still delicious with canned or frozen. Serve on its own or over rice.

Preparation Time: 20 minutes

Difficulty Level: Medium

Cooking Time: 20 minutes

Servings: 8

Ingredients:

- 1 tablespoon olive oil

- 1 onion, chopped

- 2 red bell pepper, seeded and chopped

- 1 jalapeno pepper, seeded and minced

- 10 fresh mushrooms, quartered

- 6 roman (plum) tomatoes, diced

- 1 cup of fresh corn kernels

- 1 teaspoon of ground black pepper

- 1 teaspoon of ground cumin

- 1 tablespoon of chili powder

- 2 (15 oz) cans of black beans, drained and rinsed

- 1 1/2 cups of chicken broth or vegetable broth

- 1 teaspoon of salt

Directions:

Heat oil in a large saucepan over medium to high heat, stir in the onion, red bell pepper, jalapeno, mushrooms, tomatoes, and corn for 10 minutes or until translucent onions are in, season with black pepper, cumin, and chili powder to taste, then stir in the salt and black beans, chicken, or vegetable stock. Bring them to a boil.

Reduce to medium-low heat. Remove 1 1/2 cups of soup from the food processor or blender; purée and stir the bean mixture back into the soup. Serve hot on its own or over rice.

Nutrition:

- Calories: 164 Cal

- Fat: 2.8 g

- Carbs: 28 g

- Fiber: 8 g

- Sugar: 6 g

- Protein: 9 g

- Total Fat: 2.8 g

- Cholesterol: < 1 mg

- Sodium: 897 mg

Chapter 8. Side Dishes recipes

15. Ice Cream Cake

You can use any flavor of ice cream or cake mix you like! Frost with frosting or fudge topping or thinned ice milk or anything!

Preparation Time: 25 minutes

Cooking Time: 0 minutes

Difficulty Level: Moderate

Servings: 24

Ingredients:

- ¾ quart container vanilla ice cream

- ¾ quart container chocolate ice cream

- ¼ cup hot fudge sauce

- 6 Oreo thins crushed

- ¾ cups heavy whipping cream

- ⅛ cup sugar

- ½ teaspoon vanilla

- Rainbow sprinkles

Directions

Remove the vanilla and chocolate ice cream from the freezer and defrost it for 15 minutes at room temperature;

Meanwhile, take two 8-inches cake pans and line them with a plastic sheet;

Spread the vanilla ice cream in one pan, and chocolate ice cream in the other pan, then press the ice cream to remove all the air bubbles;

Cover the ice cream and return the ice cream to the freeze. Allow it to freeze for 12 hours;

Meanwhile, beat heavy cream with vanilla and sugar in a large bowl until it makes stiff peaks;

Remove the ice cream pans from the freezer and remove the ice cream from the pans by holding their plastic sheets;

Place the chocolate ice cream layer at the bottom of a serving platter;

Top this layer with hot fudge sauce; drizzle Oreo thins on top;

Finally, place the white ice cream layer on top of it;

Spread the cream mixture over the ice cream cake;

Garnish the cake with rainbow sprinkles;

Slice and serve.

Nutrition:

- Calories: 349

- Carbs: 24g

- Fat: 13g

- Protein: 16g

Chapter 9. Sides and Salads Recipes

16.Grits

This Cracker Barrel copycat recipe for grits is one of the best you will ever find. If you've never tried grits, you will be pleasantly surprised. Try adding different kinds of cheese to make them even better.

Preparation Time: 10 minutes

Difficulty Level: Medium

Cooking Time: 30 minutes

Servings: 2

Ingredients:

- 2 cups water

- 1¼ cups milk

- 1 teaspoon salt

- 1 cup quick-cooking (not instant) grits

- ¼ cup butter

Directions:

Bring the water, milk, and salt to a boil in a small pot.

Whisk the grits into the liquid, stirring constantly until they are well combined.

Allow the mixture to return to a boil, then cover, reduce heat, and cook for about 30 minutes, stirring frequently.

Remove from heat and stir in the butter (and cheese, if desired).

Serve with butter on top.

Nutrition:

- Calories 218,

- Total Fat 90 g,

- Carbs 66 g,

- Protein 39 g,

- Sodium 2038 mg

17. Breaded Fried Okra

There are some vegetables that just scream, "I am Southern," and deep-fried okra is definitely one of them. This copycat recipe makes it easy to make at home.

Preparation Time: 10 minutes

Difficulty Level: Medium

Cooking Time: 30 minutes

Servings: 2

Ingredients:

- 1 pound fresh okra, rinsed and dried

- 1 cup self-rising cornmeal

- ½ cup self-rising flour

- 1 teaspoon salt

- 1 cup vegetable oil (for frying)

- Salt and pepper to taste

Directions:

Heat the oil in a large skillet or deep fryer.

Cut the okra into ½-inch pieces.

Combine the cornmeal, flour, and salt in a large bowl.

Drop the okra pieces into the bowl and toss to coat. Allow to rest for a few minutes while the oil heats up.

Using a slotted spoon, transfer the okra from the bowl into the hot oil. Cook for about 10 minutes or until the okra has turned a nice golden color.

Remove from oil and place on a plate lined with paper towels to drain. Season to taste with salt and pepper.

Nutrition:

- Calories 318,

- Total Fat 90 g,

- Carbs 66 g,

- Protein 39 g,

- Sodium 2038 mg

18.Pinto Beans

This Cracker Barrel copycat recipe is a great side dish to serve with any meal. The smoked ham hocks add an abundance of flavor.

Preparation Time: 10 minutes

Difficulty Level: Medium

Cooking Time: 60 minutes

Servings: 4

Ingredients:

- 1 pound ham hocks or country ham

- 1 tablespoon sugar

- 2 quarts water

- 2 cups dry pinto beans, sorted and washed

- 1½ teaspoons salt

Directions:

Cook the ham hocks until well done. Reserve the stock and pull the meat from the bone.

Remove any pebbles from the beans, rinse them, and add them to a large pot with the water. Season with salt and add the ham and reserved stock.

Bring to a boil, then reduce heat, cover and simmer for about 3 hours or until beans are tender.

Alternatively, you can add all of the ingredients (with the ham still on the bone) to a slow cooker and cook on low for 6–8 hours.

Nutrition:

- Calories 218,

- Total Fat 90 g,

- Carbs 66 g,

- Protein 39 g,

- Sodium 2038 mg

Chapter 10. Pasta recipes

19.Cheese Cake Factory's Spiced Pumpkin Cheesecake

The spices take the flavors in this pumpkin cheesecake to another level.

Preparation Time: 30 minutes

Difficulty Level: Medium

Cooking Time: 1 hour plus chilling

Servings: 12

Ingredients:

For the crust:

- 1 3/4 cups of graham cracker crumbs

- 6 tablespoons of unsalted butter, melted

- 3 tablespoons of granulated sugar

- 1/2 teaspoon of ground cinnamon powder

For the filling:

- 4 8-oz. packages of cream cheese, softened

- 1 1/2 cup of light brown sugar

- 3 large eggs

- 15 oz. can of pureed pumpkin

- 1/3 cup of heavy cream

- 1 teaspoon of vanilla extract

- 1/2 teaspoon of ground cinnamon powder

- 1/4 teaspoon of ground ginger

- 1/4 teaspoon of freshly grated nutmeg

- 1/4 teaspoon ground all spice

Directions:

Preheat oven to 350°F.

For the crust - combine crumbs, butter, sugar, and cinnamon. Press down flat into the bottom of a greased 9-inch springform pan. Bake for eight minutes and cool completely.

Beat the cream cheese and the sugar until it is fluffy. Add the eggs, the pumpkin, the heavy cream, the vanilla, and the spices and beat until blended. Add the mixture to the crust and spread it evenly.

Bake for about an hour or so. Take away from the oven and let it cool down.

Once the cake is completely cooled, cover with plastic wrap and refrigerate for at least five hours before serving.

Serving suggestion:

Serve topped with dollops of whipped cream.

Nutrition:

- Calories: 6778 Cal

- Fat: 418.53 g

- Carbs: 634.75 g

- Fiber: 80.8 g

- Sugar: 383.94 g

- Protein: 157.34 g

20.   Cheese Cake Factory's Pecan Crunch Pumpkin Cheesecake

Crunchy pecan topping adds a wonderful texture to this delicious cheesecake.

Preparation Time: 35 minutes

Cooking Time: 1 hour plus chilling time

Difficulty Level: Medium

Servings: 12

Ingredients:

For the crunch topping:

- 1 1/2 cups pecan nuts, roughly chopped

- 6 tablespoons of salted butter at room temperature.

- 1/4 cup all-purpose flour

- 1/4 cup of light brown sugar

- 1/4 teaspoon of ground cinnamon powder

- 1/4 teaspoon of salt

For the filling:

- 4 8-oz. packages of cream cheese, softened

- 1 1/2 cup of light brown sugar

- 3 large eggs

- 15 oz. can of pureed pumpkin

- 1/3 cup of heavy cream

- 1 1/2 teaspoon of vanilla extract

- 1/4 teaspoon of ground cinnamon powder

- 1/8 teaspoon of nutmeg

Directions:

Preheat oven to 350°F.

For the filling - Beat cream cheese and sugar until fluffy. Add in eggs, pumpkin, heavy cream, vanilla, and spices and beat well until combined. Pour mixture into a greased 8 by 8-inch baking dish and spread out evenly.

For the crunch topping - Combine the butter, pecans, flour, and sugar, cinnamon, and salt. Mix well together until the mixture holds but has a crumbly texture.

Scatter the topping evenly over the pumpkin mixture.

Bake for about an hour or so. Remove from the oven and let it cool down.

Once the cake has been completely cooled, cover with plastic wrap and refrigerate for at least five hours before serving.

Serving suggestion:

Serve with a glass of vanilla ice cream.

Nutrition:

- Calories: 7919 Cal

- Fat: 523.75 g

- Carbs: 687.47 g

- Fiber: 94.2 g

- Sugar: 413.49 g

- Protein: 172.37 g

Chapter 11. Pasta Recipe Part 2

21. Red Lobster's Shrimp Pasta

A recipe for Red Lobster's Shrimp Pasta made with olive oil, garlic, shrimp, clam juice or chicken broth, white wine, heavy cream, Parmesan.

Preparation Time: 5 minutes

Cooking Time: 30 minutes

Difficulty Level: Moderate

Servings: 4

Ingredients:

- 8 ozs linguini or spaghetti pasta

- ⅓ cup extra virgin olive oil

- 3 garlic cloves

- 1 pound shrimp, peeled, deveined

- ⅔ cup clam juice or chicken broth

- ⅓ cup white wine

- 1 cup heavy cream

- ½ cup parmesan cheese, freshly grated

- ¼ teaspoon dried basil, crushed

- ¼ teaspoon dried oregano, crushed

- Fresh parsley and parmesan cheese for garnish

Directions:

Cook the Pasta according to package directions. Simmer the garlic in hot oil over low heat until tender. Increase the heat to low to medium and add the shrimp. When the shrimp is cooked, transfer it to a separate bowl along with the garlic. Keep the remaining oil in the pan. Pour the clam or chicken broth into the pan and bring to a boil.

Add the wine and adjust the heat to medium. Keep cooking the mixture for another 3 minutes. While stirring the mixture, reduce the heat to low and add in the cream and cheese. Keep stirring. When the mixture thickens, return the shrimp to the pan and throw in the remaining ingredients (except the pasta). Place the pasta in a bowl and pour the sauce over it. Mix everything together and serve. Garnish with parsley and parmesan cheese, if desired.

Nutrition:

- Calories: 590

- Fat: 26 g

- Carbs: 54 g

- Protein: 34 g

- Sodium: 1500 mg

22.   Olive Garden's Steak Gorgonzola

Copycat Olive Garden Steak Gorgonzola recipe. Creamy Parmesan and Gorgonzola pasta with balsamic steak

Preparation Time: 10 minutes

Cooking Time: 1 hour and 30minutes

Difficulty Level: Moderate

Servings: 6

Ingredients:

Pasta:

- ½ pounds boneless beef top sirloin steaks, cut into ½-inch cubes

- 1 pound fettuccine or linguini, cooked

- 2 tablespoons sun-dried tomatoes, chopped

- 2 tablespoons balsamic vinegar glaze

- Some fresh parsley leaves, chopped

Marinade:

- ½ cups Italian dressing

- 1 tablespoon fresh rosemary, chopped

- 1 tablespoon fresh lemon juice (optional)

- Spinach Gorgonzola Sauce:

- 4 cups baby spinach, trimmed

- 2 cups Alfredo sauce (recipe follows)

- ½ cup green onion, chopped

- 6 tablespoons gorgonzola, crumbled, and divided)

Directions:

Cook the pasta and set aside. Mix together the marinade ingredients in a sealable container.

Marinate the beef in the container for an hour.

While the beef is marinating, make the Spinach Gorgonzola sauce. Heat the Alfredo sauce in a saucepan over medium heat. Add spinach and green onions. Let simmer until the spinach wilt. Crumble 4 tablespoons of the Gorgonzola cheese on top of the sauce. Let melt and stir. Set aside the remaining 2 tablespoons of the cheese for garnish. Set aside and cover with lid to keep warm.

When the beef is done marinating, grill each piece depending on your preference.

Toss the cooked pasta and the Alfredo sauce in a saucepan, and then transfer to a plate.

Top the pasta with the beef, and garnish with balsamic glaze, sun-dried tomatoes, gorgonzola cheese crumbles, and parsley leaves.

Serve and enjoy.

Nutrition:

- Calories: 740.5

- Fat: 27.7 g

- Carbs: 66 g

- Protein: 54.3 g

- Sodium: 848.1 mg

23. Cheesecake Factory's Pasta di Vinci

Sautéed Chicken, Mushrooms, and Onions in a Delicious Madeira Wine Sauce Tossed with Penne Pasta and Parmesan.

Preparation Time: 10 minutes

Cooking Time: 50 minutes

Difficulty Level: Easy

Servings: 4

Ingredients:

- ½ red onion, chopped

- 1 cup mushrooms, quartered

- 2 teaspoons garlic, chopped

- 1 pound chicken breast, cut into bite-size pieces

- 3 tablespoons butter, divided

- 2 tablespoons flour

- 2 teaspoons salt

- ¼ cup white wine

- 1 cup cream of chicken soup mixed with some milk

- 4 tablespoons heavy cream

- Basil leaves for serving, chopped Parmesan cheese for serving

- 1 pound penne pasta, cooked, drained

Directions:

Sauté the onion, mushrooms, and garlic in 1 tablespoon of the butter.

When they are tender, remove them from the butter and place in a bowl. Cook the chicken in the same pan. When the chicken is done, transfer it to the bowl containing the garlic, onions, and mushrooms, and set everything aside.

Using the same pan, make a roux using the flour and remaining butter over low to medium heat. When the roux is ready, mix in the salt, wine, and cream of chicken mixture. Continue stirring the mixture, making sure that it does not burn. When the mixture thickens and allow the mixture to simmer for a few more minutes. Mix in the ingredients that you set aside, and transfer the cooked pasta to a bowl or plate. Pour the sauce over the pasta, garnish with parmesan cheese and basil, and serve.

Nutrition:

- Calories: 844.9

- Fat: 35.8 g

- Carbs: 96.5 g

- Protein: 33.9 g

- Sodium: 1400.2 mg

Chapter 12. Soups recipes

24.   Cheesy Zucchini Soup

You can't wait to make this delicious, slightly spicy soup every summer when zucchini and squash are plentiful in our garden. You will like to serve this soup with warm tortillas.

Preparation Time: 5 minutes

Cooking Time: 20 minutes

Difficulty Level: Easy

Servings: 4

Ingredients:

- 3 zucchinis, cut into chunks

- 1 medium onion, peeled, chopped

- ¼ teaspoon ground black pepper

- 1 tablespoon nutritional yeast

- 1 tablespoon chopped parsley

- 2 tablespoons coconut oil

- 1 tablespoon coconut cream

- 2 cups chicken broth

Directions

Take a medium pot, place it over medium heat, add oil and when it melts, add onion and cook for 5 minutes or until softened.

Add zucchini, pour in the broth, bring it to a simmer and then cook for 15 minutes until zucchini has cooked through, covering the pot partially.

When done, stir in yeast, remove the pot from heat and then puree the soup by using an immersion blender until smooth.

Season the soup with black pepper, garnish with parsley and cream, and then serve.

Nutrition

- Calories: 108

- Fats: 8 g

- Protein: 2g

- Net Carb: 4g

- Fiber: 2g

25.   Cheddar and Bacon Soup

A rich and delightful potato soup recipe. Potatoes are cooked in the microwave, then simmered with milk, bacon, spring onions, cheese, and soured cream.

Preparation Time: 5 minutes

Cooking Time: 30 minutes

Difficulty Level: Medium

Servings: 8

Ingredients:

- 3 cups cooked chicken, cubed

- ½ cup celery, diced

- ½ of medium white onion, peeled, chopped

- 12 slices of bacon, chopped, cooked

- 1 tablespoon minced garlic

- ¼ teaspoon xanthan gum

- 1 teaspoon salt

- ½ teaspoon cayenne pepper

- ½ teaspoon ground black pepper

- 1 cup heavy whipping cream

- ¼ cup butter, unsalted

- 1 tablespoon avocado oil

- 3 cups shredded cheddar cheese

- 4 cups chicken broth

- 1 tablespoon water

Directions

Take a large pot, place it over medium heat, add onion and when hot, add celery and onion and then cook for 5 minutes.

Add butter, wait until it melts, pour in the chicken broth and then bring it to a boil.

Season the soup with salt, cayenne pepper, and black pepper, stir until mixed, switch heat to medium-low level, and then simmer for 10 minutes.

Then take a small bowl, stir together water and xanthan gum in it, and stir this mixture into the soup until combined.

Add cream and cheese, and then continue stirring until cheese has melted and blended into the soup.

Add cooked chicken pieces along with three-fourth of the bacon, stir until mixed and cook for 2 minutes until hot.

Ladle soup among four bowls, garnish with remaining bacon and more cheese and then serve.

Nutrition

- Calories: 502

- Fats: 39.6g

- Protein: 32.6g

- Net Carb: 2.75g

- Fiber: 0.25g

Chapter 13. Lunch

26.   Olive Garden Steak Gorgonzola Alfredo

The Olive Garden Steak Gorgonzola Alfredo is a recipe that so many of you have requested that I would do, so I knew this had to be a delicious recipe to try to recreate.

Preparation Time: 30 minutes

Cooking Time: 10 minutes

Servings: 2

Difficulty Level: Moderate

Ingredients:

For Steak

- 1 lb. eye of round steak medallions

- 1 tbsp. balsamic vinegar

- Pinch of salt

- Pinch of ground black pepper

Alfredo

- 1 lb. fettuccine noodles

- 2 cup heavy cream

- ¼ lb. unsalted butter

- 1¾ cup spinach

- ¼ tsp. ground nutmeg

- 1¼ cup Parmesan cheese

- Pinch of salt

- Pinch of ground black pepper

- 4-oz. gorgonzola crumbles

Toppings

- 2-oz. gorgonzola crumbles

- 3 tbsp. balsamic glaze

- ¼ cup sun-dried tomatoes

Directions:

Season the steak with salt and pepper evenly.

In a Ziploc bag, place steak and balsamic vinegar.

Seal the bag and refrigerate for at least 30 minutes or for up to 4 hours.

Heat a large, nonstick skillet over medium heat and cook steak medallions until cooked through.

Transfer the steak pieces onto a plate and, with a piece of foil, cover them.

In a pan of salted boiling water, cook fettuccine according to the package's instructions.

Drain the pasta, reserving 1 cup of the cooking liquid.

Meanwhile, in a large pan, add cream and butter over medium heat and cook until the butter is melted.

Reduce the heat to medium-low and stir in spinach and nutmeg.

Add cream mixture and cook for about 5 minutes.

Add Parmesan cheese, salt, and pepper and stir to combine.

Add the pasta and toss to coat well.

Cook for about 2-3 minutes. (You can add reserved cooking liquid if the mixture is too thick).

Remove from the heat and stir in gorgonzola cheese.

Divide pasta mixture into onto plates and top with the steak medallions, balsamic glaze, sun-dried tomatoes, and the gorgonzola crumbles.

Nutrition:

- Calories: 250

- Carbs: 38g

- Fat: 7g

- Protein: 10g

27.   Olive Garden Bolognese Sauce Recipe

Olive Garden Three Meat Sauce combines ground beef, Italian sausage, and pepperoni to make a meat sauce recipe perfect for any pasta dish. You know Olive Garden has the best pasta sauces, and this one doesn't disappoint. In fact, I think you will find this one of the best spaghetti sauces you can make at home.

Preparation Time: 2 minutes

Cooking Time: 1 hour and 15 minutes

Servings:

Difficulty Level: Moderate

Ingredients:

- 2 tbsp. olive oil

- 1½ carrot, chopped finely

- 1 celery stalk, chopped finely

- 1 onion, chopped finely

- 3 garlic cloves, chopped finely

- ½ lb. ground beef

- 6-oz. Italian sausage, skinned

- 1 cup red wine

- 1 (28-oz.) can tomatoes, chopped and crushed

- 1 tsp. fresh sage, chopped

- 1 tsp. fresh rosemary, chopped

- Salt and ground black pepper, to taste

Directions:

In a large pan, heat oil over medium heat and cook carrot, celery, onion, and garlic for about 5 minutes.

Add beef and sausage and cook for about 10 minutes, stirring occasionally.

Stir in wine and cook until reduced by half.

Stir in remaining ingredients and simmer for about 1 hour before serving.

Nutrition:

- Calories: 297

- Carbs: 5g

- Fat: 19g

- Protein: 24g

Chapter 14. Dinner

28.   Meatloaf

This is a very easy and no-fail recipe for meatloaf. It won't take long to make at all, and it's quite good!

Preparation Time: 30 minutes

Cooking Time: 45 minutes

Servings: 4

Difficulty Level: Easy

Ingredients:

- Onion (1)

- Green pepper (1)

- Ground beef (1 lb.)

- Diced tomatoes (1 can)

- Egg (1)

- Frozen biscuits - grated (.5 cup)

- Salt (1 tsp.)

- Ketchup (.25 cup)

Directions:

Set the oven temperature at 350° Fahrenheit.

Use a box grater to prepare the frozen biscuits. Dice the onions and peppers.

Combine all of the fixings (omit the ketchup).

Lightly spritz a loaf pan using a cooking oil spray. Add the beef mixture. Bake the meatloaf for one hour and 15 minutes.

Transfer the baking tray from the oven and wait for about ten minutes.

Drain the juices from the pan and place the meatloaf onto a serving platter.

Garnish the meatloaf with ketchup and serve.

Nutrition:

- Calories: 232

- Carbs: 3g

- Fat: 25g

- Protein: 29g

29. Loaded Potato Salad

This is an unusual recipe for potato salad. It is a switch from your everyday mayonnaise-based salad. It's like a baked potato in a bowl!

Preparation Time: 10 minutes

Cooking Time: 25 minutes

Servings: 3 - 4

Difficulty Level: Easy

Ingredients:

- Cooked potatoes (3 large)

- Hard-boiled eggs (3)

- Minced onion (4 tbsp.)

- Black pepper (as desired)

- Dry mustard (1 tsp.)

- Salt (1 tsp.)

- The Saucepan:

- Eggs (2 uncooked)

- Sugar (3 tsp.)

- Melted butter (3 tbsp.)

- Hot vinegar (.5 cup)

- Mayonnaise (1 cup)

Directions:

Mix the potatoes, eggs, onion, mustard, salt, and pepper.

Measure and add the sugar, vinegar, eggs, and melted butter in a saucepan and simmer until thickened.

Combine with the mayonnaise and served.

Nutrition:

- Calories: 240

- Carbs: 2g

- Fat: 23g

- Protein: 32g

Chapter 15. Appetizers & Snacks recipes

30.   Marinara Sauce

Homemade marinara is almost as fast and tastes immeasurably better than even the best supermarket sauce — and it's made with basic pantry ingredients.

Preparation Time: 5 minutes

Cooking Time: 30 minutes

Servings: 8

Difficulty Level: Easy

Ingredients:

- 2 Tablespoons Extra Virgin Olive Oil

- 2 scallions (white & green part) finely chopped

- 1 small yellow onion, finely chopped

- 4 Garlic cloves, minced

- 1/4 cup of hearty red wine (such as Citra Montepulciano)

- 1 Can (28 oz.) Whole tomatoes in juice

- 1 teaspoon dried oregano

- 1/2 teaspoon Crushed, Red Pepper Flakes

- 1/4 teaspoon Ground Black Pepper,

Directions:

Add the onion in the oil, and cook for about 5 minutes, occasionally stirring, until translucent. Add the anchovies, scallions (if used), garlic, and cook. Stir regularly until about 1 minute of fragrant garlic.

Swirl in wine. Pour the tomatoes into a bowl and their juices. Crush the tomatoes between your fingers, then pour the mixture into the casserole. Add the oregano, flakes of hot pepper, pepper, and bring to a simmer. Diminish heat to med. - low. Simmer, stirring regularly, until the tomato juices have thickened and the sauce is reduced slightly for 30 minutes.

Nutrition

- Calories 156

- Total Fat 6g 8 %

- Saturated Fat 2.8g 14 %

- Cholesterol 30mg 10 %

- Sodium 371mg 16 %

- Dietary Fiber 1.4g 5 %

- Sugar 4.2

- Protein 8g 16 %

31.Shrimp Scampi

Shrimp Scampi can be enjoyed as an appetizer/light meal OR for dinner with your favorite pasta of choice!

Preparation Time: 5 minutes

Cooking Time: 10 minutes

Servings: 6

Difficulty Level: Easy

Ingredients:

- 2 lbs. (approximately 15 pcs) large shrimps, peeled.

- 2 Unsalted butter sticks, chilled and melted

- 3⁄4 cup unflavored (plain) bread crumbs

- 2 tabs of dry white wine

- 3 garlic cloves, peeled and finely chopped

- 2 large spring onions

- 1 handful of fresh, flat-leaf peas, roughly chopped

- 1⁄4 cup freshly squeezed lemon juice

- 1/4 tabs of Italian seasoning

- ½ tabs garlic power

- ½ tabs onion salt

- ½ tabs dried oregano

- ½ tabs dried basil

- Salt and pepper

Directions

Lay the shrimps in a big, oven-safe casserole dish. Season with pepper and salt. Place it on aside.

Prepare a large mug. Mix melted butter, lemon juice, dry white wine in a cup, and minced garlic. Blend well. Add the spring onion chopped in the white portion and the chopped flat-leaf parsley.

Pour the butter mixture uniformly over the shrimps. Make sure every part of the shrimp has the mixture well coated. Put it on for 30 minutes.

Prepare one bigger bowl. Mix the crumbs of bread, the salt of onion, the garlic powder, the dried oregano, the dried basil, and the Italian seasoning. Blend well.

Coat the breadcrumb mixture evenly over the shrimp until the shrimp surface is completely covered.

Bake the shrimp 10 minutes in the oven. The shrimp will turn golden brown and thicken and bubble the butter sauce. If you like the butter sauce flavor, you don't need to make a recycle of the Carrabba's lemon butter sauce.

Remove from the oven, and serve while hot.

Nutrition

- Calories from Fat 270

- Calories 700 46%

- Total Fat 30g 55%

- Saturated Fat 11g

- Trans Fat 0g 50%

- Protein 31g

Chapter 16. Sauces & Glazes recipes

32.   Chili's Chicken Mushroom Soup

This is a delicious root vegetable soup recipe, sure to warm you up on a chilly day.

Difficulty Level: Easy

Preparation Time: 10 minutes

Cooking Time: 30

Servings: 6-8

Ingredients:

- ¼ cup (½ stick) butter

- ¼ cup diced carrots

- ¼ cup diced celery

- ¼ cup diced yellow onions

- ½ cup flour

- 3 cups sliced mushrooms

- 5½ cups chicken broth

- ¼ teaspoon thyme

- Pinch of dried tarragon

- ½ teaspoon hot pepper sauce

- 1 teaspoon black pepper

- 1 teaspoon chopped fresh parsley

- ¾ pound cooked and diced chicken

- 1½ teaspoons lemon juice

- 3 cups half-and-half

Directions:

Melt the butter over medium heat into a big soup pot.

Add the vegetables and sauté until tender, for 4-5 minutes.

Pour in the flour and keep mixing.

Add the chicken broth gradually.

Add herbs, pepper, pepper sauce, and parsley to the pot and mix well. Simmer on for ten minutes.

Mix the half-and-a-half, lemon juice, and chicken. Allow to simmer and boil for 10 minutes.

Nutrition

- Calories: 3257 Cal

- Fat: 150g

- Carbs: 133g

- Fiber: 12.7 g

Chapter 17. Sauces and Dressings

33.   Caramel Sauce

Preparation Time: 5 minutes

Cooking Time: 15 minutes

Difficulty Level: Easy

Servings: 12

Ingredients:

- 3 tablespoons erythritol sweetener

- 1 teaspoon vanilla extract, unsweetened

- 1/3 cup butter, salted

- 2/3 cup heavy cream

Directions

Take a medium saucepan, place it over low heat, add butter and erythritol and then cook for 4 to 5 minutes until butter melts and turns golden brown.

Stir in cream, bring it to a gentle boil and then simmer the sauce for 10 minutes until the sauce has thickened to coat the back of the spoon, stirring constantly.

Remove pan from heat, stir in vanilla extract and then serve.

Nutrition:

- Calories: 91

- Fats: 10g

- Protein: 1g

- Net Carb: 0g

- Fiber: 1g

34.   Paula Deen BBQ Sauce

Barbecue Sauce for your all-purpose barbecue needs.

Preparation Time: 5 minutes

Cooking Time: 5 minutes

Difficulty Level: Easy

Servings: 32

Ingredients:

- 1 teaspoon onion powder

- 1 teaspoon salt

- ½ teaspoon cayenne pepper

- 1 teaspoon ground black pepper

- ¾ cup erythritol sweetener

- 2 teaspoons paprika

- ½ teaspoon cinnamon

- 2 tablespoons mustard paste

- ½ teaspoon xanthan gum

- 3 tablespoons lemon juice

- 1 ½ tablespoons liquid smoke

- ½ cup apple cider vinegar

- ¾ cup ketchup, low-carb

- 1 tablespoon Worcestershire sauce

- ½ cup of water

Directions

Take a medium saucepan, place it over medium heat, add mustard, Worcestershire sauce, liquid smoke, and ketchup in it, and then pour in vinegar, lemon juice, and water.

Whisk until combined, cook it for 3 to 4 minutes until sauce begins to bubbles, and then whisk in xanthan gum until incorporated.

Then add erythritol and all the spices, whisk until combined, and remove the pan from heat.

Let the sauce cool completely, then serve immediately or store it in an air-tight jar or squeeze bottle.

Nutrition:

- Calories: 10

- Fats: 2g

- Protein: 0g

- Net Carb: 2g

- Fiber: 0g

Chapter 18. Desserts recipes

35.   Chocolate Brownie Lasagna

Who knew sweet and savory could result in this dessert lasagna? Olive Garden sure did.

Preparation Time: 15 minutes

Cooking Time: 60 minutes

Servings: 8

Difficulty Level: Medium

Ingredients:

Cake

- 6 cups cake flour, sifted

- 5¼ cups sugar

- 2¼ cups Hershey's cocoa

- 2 tablespoons baking soda

- 4½ cups milk

- 1½ cups butter

- 1 dozen large eggs

- 1 tablespoon vanilla extract

- 2 cups semi-sweet chocolate chips

Buttercream

- ⅔ cup water

- ¼ cup meringue powder

- 12 cups confectioners' sugar, sifted

- 1¼ cups shortening

- ¾ teaspoon salt

- 1 teaspoon clear almond extract

- 1 teaspoon clear vanilla extract

- 1 teaspoon colorless butter flavor

Directions

To make the cake, preheat the oven to 350°F. Grease three 10-inch springform pans with cooking spray.

Stir the sifted cake flour, sugar, cocoa, and baking soda into a mixing bowl. Add the butter and combine. Add the eggs, vanilla, and milk. Mix thoroughly.

Transfer about 5 cups of cake batter into the pans. Bake for 40–50 minutes or until an inserted toothpick comes out clean. Cool for 10 minutes before removing from pans.

Make the buttercream by using an electric mixer to whip the water and meringue powder at high speed until peaks form.

Slowly add 4 cups of sugar. Beat at low speed. Add the shortening and then the remainder of the sugar. Add the salt and flavorings and continue to beat at low speed until smooth.

Thin out half of the frosting with some water. (This will be used to fill layers between the cakes.)

Assemble by placing one cake on a platter. Spread thinned frosting on top. Sprinkle with some semi-sweet chocolate chips, then top with the second layer of cake. Frost the top of the second layer with the thinned frosting. Place the third layer of cake on top. Frost the top with the remaining buttercream and sprinkle with more chocolate chips.

Cut into wedges and serve.

Nutrition:

- Calories: 235;

- Carbs: 23g;

- Protein: 12g;

- Fats: 45g;

36.　　Provencal apple pie with walnuts

This Apple Walnut Pie recipe is made from scratch. Super easy to make. Just 9 ingredients and 20 minutes of active prep time. Perfect for Thanksgiving.

Preparation Time: 15 minutes

Cooking Time: 30 minutes

Servings: 8

Difficulty Level: Moderate

Ingredients:

- Egg white - 2 pieces

- Cane sugar - ½ cup

- Vanilla extract - 1 teaspoon

- Baking powder - 1 teaspoon

- Ground cinnamon - ½ teaspoon

- Wheat flour - ½ cup

- Walnuts - 35 g

- An Apple - 2 pieces

Preparation

Peel the apples, cut it into half, and remove the core. Cut into small cubes.

Preheat the oven to 180 degrees. Butter a small baking pan or pan.

In a bowl, beat the whites, vanilla, sugar, baking powder, and cinnamon. Then add flour, nuts, and apples. Mix well.

Transfer the dough into the prepared form and bake for 30 minutes until cooked.

Nutrition:

- Calories: 310;

- Carbs:12 g;

- Protein: 23g;

- Fats: 3.4 g;

Chapter 19. Snacks

37. Wulfs apple pie

Classic Apple Pie Recipe with an irresistible homemade apple pie filling. From the best flaky pie crust to the generous saucy center, this recipe always gets glowing reviews. This is the pie everyone has to make for Thanksgiving!

Preparation Time: 5 minutes

Cooking Time: 10 minutes

Servings: 6

Difficulty Level: Moderate

Ingredients:

- Puff pastry - 500 g

- Sour cream 20% - 400 g

- Honey - 100 g

- Chicken egg - 2 pieces

- An Apple - 5 items

- Butter - 50 g

- Cinnamon – taste

Directions

Roll out the puff pastry; put it in a baking sheet. Fry the apples in butter until soft, add honey, cinnamon, mix and remove from heat.

Lightly beat the sour cream with two eggs and mix with apples. Put apples and sour cream on rolled dough; wrap the edges of the dough. Lubricate with the remaining beaten egg and place for thirty to forty minutes in the oven, heated to 200 degrees.

Nutrition:

- Calories: 676

- Carbs:12 g;

- Protein: 23g;

- Fats: 41 g;

Chapter 20. Beverages, Drinks & Coffee recipes

38.   Screaming Red Zombie from Red Robin

The Red Robin Screaming Red Zombie drink may be strong enough to revive the dead, but it is also a great way to cool off on a hot day.

Preparation Time: 7 minutes

Cooking Time: 0 minutes

Servings: 1

Difficulty Level: Moderate

Ingredients:

- Three ozs of orange juice

- Four ozs of lemon juice

- Half-oz each of

- Bacardi Select Ram

- Myer's Dark Rum

- Grenadine

- One tbsp. of sugar

- One oz of light rum

Directions:

Use a bowl to make a mixture of lemon juice and sugar.

Then, mix one oz of rum and orange juice with mixture lemon juice. Stir the mixture to blend completely.

Fill the ice into the half part of the cup, measuring 16 ozs.

Pour the mixture over the ice containing cup.

Use a spoon to float to mix all the three ingredients required in half-ozs each.

Enjoy the drink immediately after serving it.

Nutrition:

- Calories: 257;

- Carbs: 35 g;

- Protein: 5g;

- Fats: 12g;

- Fiber: 1g

Chapter 21. Nutritious Fish and Seafood Main Entrees

39.   Linguine with Anchovies and Mushrooms

An Olive Garden copycat that elevates the saltiness of anchovies for an easy but fancy pasta dish.

Preparation Time: 30 minutes

Cooking Time: 30 minutes

Servings: 4

Difficulty Level: Easy

Ingredients:

- ½ cup extra-virgin olive oil

- 2 tablespoons fresh garlic, minced

- ¼ cup (2 ozs) anchovy fillets packed in olive oil, drained

- 2 pounds mussels in shells, rinsed and cleaned

- 1 cup white wine

- 1 pound linguine pasta

- ½ cup pine nuts, toasted

- ¼ cup parsley, chopped

Directions:

Heat the olive oil in a skillet over low heat. Add the garlic and anchovies. Sauté until garlic is golden brown, and anchovies turn to a paste.

Add the mussels and white wine. Simmer on medium heat until the mussels open, stirring frequently.

Cook the linguine according to package directions. Drain, then mix into the skillet with the sauce.

Transfer to a serving plate. Garnish with pine nuts and parsley. Serve.

Nutrition:

- Calories: 219

- Fat: 17 g

- Saturated fat: 10 g

- Carbs: 28 g

- Sugar: 7 g

- Fibers: 1 g

- Protein: 17 g

- Sodium: 1134 mg

Chapter 22. Chicken and Fish Recipes

40.　　　Farm-Raised Catfish

Good ol' southern-fried catfish! This is another traditional Southern dish that Cracker Barrel does right. It's so full of flavor, it is a menu favorite, and this copycat recipe is so close to the menu item that it will hold you over until you can get to the restaurant.

Preparation Time: 10 minutes

Cooking Time: 45 minutes

Servings: 4

Difficulty Level: Moderate

Ingredients:

- ¼ cup all-purpose flour

- ¼ cup cornmeal

- 1 teaspoon onion powder

- 1 teaspoon dried basil

- ½ teaspoon garlic salt

- ½ teaspoon dried thyme

- ¼–½ teaspoon white pepper

- ¼–½ teaspoon cayenne pepper

- ¼–½ teaspoon black pepper

- 4 catfish fillets (6–8 ozs each)

- ¼ cup butter

Directions:

Add the flour, cornmeal, onion powder, basil, salt, thyme, white pepper, cayenne pepper, and black pepper to a large plastic freezer bag.

Place the catfish fillets in the bag and gently shake to coat. Fish breaks easily, so be careful!

Heat a large skillet over medium-high heat. Add the butter, and when it melts, lay in the catfish. Cook, covered, for 8–10 minutes on each side, or until the fish flakes easily with a fork.

Nutrition:

- Calories: 112

- Total Fat: 23g

- Carbs: 12g

- Protein: 81g

- Fiber: 0g

41.Lemon Pepper Trout

Cracker Barrel's lemon pepper trout is a wonderful dish. This copycat recipe pays tribute to the original from the restaurant.

Preparation Time: 10 minutes

Cooking Time: 15 minutes

Servings: 4

Difficulty Level: Moderate

Ingredients:

- 6 (4-oz) trout fillets

- 3 tablespoons butter, melted

- 2 medium lemons, thinly sliced

- 2 tablespoons lemon juice

Sauce

- 3 tablespoons butter

- ¼ teaspoon pepper

- 2 tablespoons lemon juice

Directions:

Melt the butter in a saucepan over low heat and allow it to cook until it begins to brown (don't burn it). Add the pepper and lemon juice.

Brush the fish fillets with melted butter. Lay lemon slices on top of each.

If cooking on a grill, use a wire grilling basket sprayed with nonstick cooking spray. Grill for about 10 minutes or until the fish flakes easily with a fork.

Alternatively, you can bake in a 350°F oven for 10–15 minutes.

Transfer to a serving platter and top with additional lemon slices.

Serve with the butter lemon sauce you made.

Nutrition:

- Calories: 111

- Total Fat: 23g

- Carbs: 12g

- Protein: 81g

- Fiber: 0g

Chapter 23. Favorite Copycat Recipes

42.   Texas Roadhouse Steak Rub

Just a few simple seasonings are all you want to make the quality dry steak rub recipe to complement the exquisite flavors in your chicken or steak, and style like the Texas Roadhouse restaurant! It is a perfect summertime grilling spice rub.

Difficulty Level: Medium

Preparation Time: 30 minutes

Cooking Time: 20 minutes

Servings: 1

Ingredients:

- 1.5 tablespoons of coarse kosher salt

- 2 teaspoons of brown sugar

- 1/4 teaspoon of cornstarch

- 1/4 teaspoon of garlic powder

- 1/4 teaspoon of onion powder

- 1/4 teaspoon of turmeric

- 1/2 teaspoon of paprika

- 1/2 teaspoon of chili powder

- 1 teaspoon of black pepper powder

Directions:

In a gallon-sized plastic jar, combine all the ingredients and seal tightly. Shake it to combine all ingredients thoroughly.

Dust the steak generously with seasoning on each side and let it relax for about 40 minutes. It lets in the salt to bypass through the floor (by osmosis) and eventually helps break down the muscle fibers, which ends in extra gentle meat. At the start, the liquid seemed in the course of this length has time to reabsorb, which renders the meat juicer.

If the grill is satisfactory and hot, put the steak(s) on and cook for 4-5 minutes, until it's browned and slightly charred. Flip over and cook for a further:

5 minutes: Medium Rare

7 minutes: Medium

10 minutes: Well Cooked

Nutrition:

- Calories: 1260;

- Carbs: 32 g;

- Protein: 32g;

- Fats: 65 g;

43.   Texas Roadhouse Rolls

These Texas Roadhouse rolls are completely irresistible. They're proper for big family reunions, like Thanksgiving. Serve something warm and delicious with this recipe.

Difficulty Level: Easy

Preparation Time: 15 minutes

Cooking Time: 20 minutes

Servings: 8

Ingredients:

- 2 cups of milk

- One packet of dry yeast

- 1/2 cup of warm water

- 1/2 cup of sugar

- 1/2 cup of honey

- 7 halves of cups of flour

- Three spoonsful of butter divided, plus round one spoonful of brushing on finished rolls

- Three eggs

- Two teaspoons of salt

Directions:

Prepare one wide baking sheet (half-sheet size) or two slices of cookies with rimmed edges by using mild greasing.

Hot the milk in the microwave till on contact it is warm. While milk is heating, put yeast, heat water, and one tablespoon of sugar in a heavy-duty mixer's bowl and permit "proof" for about 5 minutes until it is foamy.

Place the ultimate sugar, honey, heat milk, and three 1⁄2 cups of flour into the mixer and use the paddle fastener to beat medium-low (setting three on a heavy-duty mixer) for 2 minutes, scrape the facets before adding butter, eggs, and milk. Beat some other 2 minutes, then crawl returned down.

With the machine walking at medium-low, step by step, add every other 2 cups of flour till the dough starts evolved, leaving the aspects of the pot. Keep the mixer down and let the dough stand for three minutes.

Beat the dough once more at medium-low, to "knead it" for 5 minutes. Put a tablespoon of flour at a time earlier than simply starts maintaining its form, and is not too sticky.

Grease a wide bowl with vegetable oil and greased fingers, get rid of the dough from the mixer bowl, and into the greased bowl, roll it in the bowl to spread the oil on the surface. Cover with plastic wrap, then lay a material towel over and enable forty-five minutes or until double in dimension to upward shove in a warm place.

Powder a surface of work gently with any ultimate flour and roll the dough out onto the surface. Knead the dough, pressure it down to deflate it, for about 1 minute, earlier than coming together in a very clean disk. To roll the dough into a huge rectangle about $1/2$-inch-thick, use a rolling pin that is gently dusted with flour. Pull the dough into two pieces, one-inch-thick, to fold. Roll once more till all layers keep tightly together. To reduce 2-inch squares, use a sharp knife or dough scraper and lay them on the organized baking sheet(s), solely barely touching every other.

Cover once more with plastic wrap and a material towel and give another hour or until double in size to grow.

You need to heat the oven to 350 F. Bake the rolls until golden brown on the pinnacle for about 25 minutes. Take out the pan(s) from the oven and brush the closing butter tablespoon all over the tops immediately.

Nutrition:

- Calories: 2246;

- Carbs: 2 g;

- Protein: 33g;

- Fats: 64 g;

Chapter 24. Popular Copycat Recipes

44.   Chicken Fried Rice

Chicken fried rice is the comfort dish of Chinese food. It's been around for a very long time and is also common in East, Southeast, and South Asian cuisines.

Preparation Time: 10 minutes

Cooking Time: 15 minutes

Servings: 4

Difficulty Level: Easy

Ingredients:

- 2 cups frozen cauliflower, curly 1 large green onion, sliced

- 1 pound skinless chicken breast, ½ cubic inch

- ¼ cup frozen peas

- 1 ½ teaspoon salt

- 1 teaspoon ground black pepper

- ½ teaspoon garlic powder

- 1 teaspoon grated ginger

- 2 teaspoons of erythritol sweetener

- 3 tablespoons unsalted butter, divided

- 3 tablespoons of coconut amino acids 2 beaten eggs

- ½ teaspoon crushed red pepper flakes

- 2 tablespoons toasted sesame oil

Directions

Take a large skillet, place on medium-high heat, add 1 tablespoon of butter and, once melted, add the beaten eggs, season with 1/3 teaspoon salt and ¼ teaspoon black pepper, then cook 2 minutes until just cooked through.

Transfer the eggs to a plate, add 1 tablespoon of butter to the pan, and when it melts, add the chicken pieces.

Add half of each garlic, ginger, and red pepper flakes, season

½ teaspoon salt and black pepper, then cook for 6 minutes until cooked.

Transfer the chicken to a plate, then add 1 tablespoon of butter to the pan and when it melts, add the peas, cauliflower, and green onion, then add the garlic flakes, ginger, and pepper remaining red.

Season with the rest of the salt and black pepper, cook for 5 minutes until the vegetables are completely hot and tender, then add the sesame oil and soy sauce.

Return the chicken and eggs to the pan, stir until combined, and cook 2 minutes until heated through.

Decorate the rice and the chicken with a little more green onion, then serve.

Nutrition:

- Calories: 324;

- Carbs: 2 g;

- Protein: 32g;

- Fats: 35 g;

- Carbohydrates 2.8g;

- Fiber 3g

45.   Mc Donald's Big Mac Bite

The Big Mac, made infamous by McDonald's. "Pickles, onions, special sauce, on a sesame seed bun" - remember? No bun here, but you get the idea. Make up plenty for leftovers, you can mix and match your favorite toppings. Who doesn't like food on a stick!? Enjoy!

Preparation Time: 15 minutes

Cooking Time: 15 minutes

Servings: 16

Difficulty Level: Easy

Ingredients:

For bites:

- ¼ cup chopped white onion

- 1½ pounds ground beef

- 1 teaspoon salt

- 16 pickle slices

- 4 slices of American cheese

- 16 lettuce leaves

For the sauce

- 4 tablespoons pickled pickles

- 1 teaspoon onion powder

- 1 teaspoon garlic powder

- 1 teaspoon paprika

- 1 teaspoon white wine vinegar

- 2 tablespoons mustard paste

- ½ cup mayonnaise

Directions

Turn on the oven, then set it to 400 degrees F and let it preheat.

During this time, prepare the bites and for this, take a large bowl, place the meat, add the onion and salt, then stir until homogeneous.

Form the mixture into sixteen balls, then press lightly to flatten the balls into patties.

Arrange the empanadas on a large baking sheet lined with a sheet of parchment and bake for 15 minutes until cooked through, turning halfway.

In the meantime, prepare the sauce and for this, take a medium bowl, put all your ingredients, then mix until homogeneous.

Once the patties are cooked, remove the baking sheet from the oven, then drain the excess fat.

Assemble the bites and for this, cut each slice of American cheese into four squares, place each square of cheese on each patty, return the baking sheet to the oven and wait until the cheese is melted.

Meanwhile, cut the lettuce into squares and when the cheese melts, cover each patty with lettuce squares and a pickle slice, then fix the bite by inserting a skewer through it.

Serve the bite with the prepared sauce.

Nutrition:

- Calories: 182;

- Carbs: 23 g;

- Protein: 10g;

- Fats: 35 g;

Chapter 25. Others

46.   Outback Steakhouse Charcoal Ribeye

There's nothing more delicious than a grilled steak and lobster dinner. While you can dine out and enjoy this delicious meal in a restaurant, it's much more cost-effective to make this dinner at home.

Preparation Time: 10 minutes

Cooking Time: 10 minutes

Servings: 4

Difficulty Level: Moderate

Ingredients:

- 4 ribeye steaks, fat trimmed, cut into 1 ½-inch thick slices

- 2 teaspoons salt

- 2 teaspoons ground black pepper

- For the Seasoning:

- 2 tablespoon erythritol sweetener

- 1 teaspoon turmeric powder

- 2 teaspoon smoked paprika

- 1 teaspoon red chili powder

- 4 tablespoons steak seasoning

Directions

Prepare the steak and for this, bring it to room temperature and then season well with salt and black pepper.

Prepare the grill by lighting the charcoals, place the cooking grate in it, cover the grill with its lid, and let it preheat for 5 minutes.

Brush the grate with oil generously, then place a prepared steak onto hottest the cooking grate and sear it for 3 minutes.

Then flip the steak, continue grilling for 3 minutes, transfer it to the warmer side of the cooking grate, and repeat with the remaining steaks.

Then shut the grill with its lid and continue cooking the steak until it has cooked to the desired doneness.

When done, remove steaks from the grill, cover them with foil and let them rest for 5 minutes.

Cut the steak into slices across the grain and then serve.

Nutrition:

- Calories: 629;

- Carbs: 8g;

- Protein: 58g;

- Fats: 41g;

- Fiber: 1g

Chapter 26. Cooking Conversion Chart (volume, temperature, ...)

. Measuring Equivalent Chart

Type	Imperial	Imperial	Metric
Weight	1 dry oz		28g
	1 pound	16 dry ozs	0.45 kg
Volume	1 teaspoon		5 ml
	1 dessert spoon	2 teaspoons	10 ml
	1 tablespoon	3 teaspoons	15 ml
	1 Australian tablespoon	4 teaspoons	20 ml
	1 fluid oz	2 tablespoons	30 ml
	1 cup	16 tablespoons	240 ml

	1 cup	8 fluid ozs	240 ml
	1 pint	2 cups	470 ml
	1 quart	2 pints	0.95 l
	1 gallon	4 quarts	3.8 l
Length	1 inch		2.54 cm

* Numbers are rounded to the closest equivalent

2. Oven Temperature Equivalent Chart

Fahrenheit (°F)	Celsius (°C)	Gas Mark
220	100	
225	110	1/4
250	120	1/2
275	140	1
300	150	2
325	160	3
350	180	4
375	190	5
400	200	6

425	220	7
450	230	8
475	250	9
500	260	

* Celsius (°C) = T (°F)-32] * 5/9

** Fahrenheit (°F) = T (°C) * 9/5 + 32

*** Numbers are rounded to the closest equivalent

Conclusion

These recipes are the perfect additions to your daily meals. If you want affordable restaurant-style food, then here is the answer.

We've got recipes from all your favorite restaurants—and then some. If you ever host a party, there are dishes in here that will make your guests ask, "Hey, what's the recipe for that chicken you served?" If you regularly cook for yourself or your family, then these simple recipes will help you elevate your meals. And if you just love having restaurant food at home, and then try making some yourself—you never know you might even be a better cook!

Italian Ingredients

Italian cooking is loaded with simple yet exciting flavors. It is well-known for wholesome Ingredients that make the meals tasty as well as healthy.

Olive Oil

Olive oil is consumed in large quantities in Italy and is called "golden liquid" in Italian cooking. Without olive oil, the most popular Italian recipes are incomplete. Loaded with monounsaturated fatty acids and noted for its anti-inflammatory properties, extra virgin olive oil provides abundant health benefits and plays a vital role in many Mediterranean recipes.

Cheese

The love for cheese in Italian cooking is incredible. Cheeses like pecorino, burrata, Parmesan, mascarpone, ricotta, and mozzarella make their appearance not only in internationally famous pizzas and pasta dishes but in everything from appetizers and salads to desserts, toasted breads, and other baked recipes.

Tomatoes

Tomato is another essential ingredient for Italian cooking. Every amazing spaghetti and pizza sauce has some tomato in it. Tomato is used in abundance during winter, but Italians make good use of all the different seasonal varieties.

Basil

Basil is highly appreciated in Mediterranean cooking and is used in many soups and salads. Pesto sauce prepared from basil makes an ideal complement to fish and poultry meals, breads, pasta, and potato dishes.

Pasta

Pasta is the pride of Italian food culture. For Italians, pasta is not just about macaroni, spaghetti, or even tagliatelle. Italians eat multiple kinds of short pasta, long pasta, baked pasta, stuffed pasta, and so on. Popular pasta varieties include fusilli, ravioli, macaroni, spaghetti, fettuccine, penne, pappardelle, and tagliatelle.

Meat & Prosciutto

Usually accompanied by legumes and fresh vegetables, Italian meat courses may be poultry, pork, lamb, or beef. Dry-cured ham products from Italy are popular in many countries. Prosciutto is used in many pasta dishes, pizzas, and other main course meals.

Oregano & Rosemary

Rosemary is treated like the queen of herbs in Italian cuisine. Its delightful aroma features most commonly in risotto, pasta, and salads. A sprinkle of dried oregano adds flavor to many pizza, salad, and pasta recipes. It is also used to give an aromatic touch in many sauces.

Garlic

Known for its medicinal properties, garlic shines as the star that makes Italian cooking more aromatic and healthier.

Jarred garlic is avoided, and fresh garlic is preferred to add more flavor.

Porcini Mushrooms

Mushrooms are often referred to as "piglets" in Italian. Italian vegetarian recipes use mushrooms in abundance to provide a meat-like texture and enhance the flavor profile. They are also used in vegetarian and non-vegetarian risotto, soup, stew, and polenta recipes.

By cooking at home, you get to save money and time, you get to control portions, and you get to customize each meal. Remember, the recipes here are more of a guide—ultimately, you get to choose how your upcoming meal will taste and how best to prepare it.

Just a quick reminder to download our other selections from the series. I hope you enjoy them!